Freedom... Seems like this mythical abstract of an idea to most people but an actuality freedom shouldn't be a choice, it's our birthright, it is something that was given to us from the beginning of time. So, the question is, why doesn't it feel that way? Well here is your answer, the truth is the way society is set up its kind of hard to become free. With the constant pressure of keeping up with the latest trends, more job promotions, new car pressure, the pressure of needing more and more just to impress people that you don't even know its kind of hard to see that we all have the option to opt out.

We have the option to decide that enough is enough and we can live a life of true meaning, purpose and freedom if we chose because as mentioned before it is our birthright. So, what exactly is freedom? Great question! Freedom is the option of choice, the option to live your life the way God intended for it to be lived. Freedom means to live a life without limitations. To find that thing you believe you were called here on this earth to do and simply do it. Freedom is the ability to drown out everyone else's stinking opinions of you and for the first time in your life take control of your life. Freedom is to have unlimited financial resources and to live a life without financial stress.

But, there lies the problem we don't know how to be FREE because most of us aren't FREE.

This is why Jake created Operation 26, an initiative to help free 260,000 families from the claws of Financial Cancer. Jake believes an educated family makes educated decisions, however when financial cancer is celebrated and very much a part of the societal norm. The thought of true freedom is almost like a dream you know will never come true.

This book was created to help you realize for yourself how sick we really are. Freedom is our birthright however we chose to turn in our rights to freedom to creditors, governments and financial institutions; just so they can give us one more hit of fantasy. Allowing us to climb further and further into debt, until financial cancer consume us, and we are their slaves for generations to come.

Is this the life you truly signed up for? A life of lies, deception and a false sense of freedom. Or do you want to learn how to break yourself free from financial cancer forever and live a life of true freedom. If the second option is you than the information in this book will be the keys you need to taken back control of your life.

TABLE OF CONTENTS

Part I
A SICK WORLD

THE PLAGUE

"THEY FANCIED THEMSELVES FREE, AND NO ONE WILL EVER BE FREE SO LONG AS THERE ARE PESTILENCES."
-ALBERT CAMUS

Are we in the midst of a plague? This is a very valid question. People are sick and have been for a very long time. If you look at the history of plagues, they sweep in and literally destroy families, leaving behind a diseased mess, holding survivors hostage and responsible for cleaning up what was left. The worst part about a plague isn't what most think; most believe the worst portion of any plague is the obvious big three: sickness, turmoil, and death. Although these three are very significant in their effects on a community, they do not top the number one most frightening factor of every plague ever recorded. The most frightening aspect of a plague is that it is typically an infectious disease that is spread either in the air, or by direct contact. You usually don't know who's infected until the disease grabs a hold of you and your family; by then it's too late. Fortunately, because of modern medicine, those illnesses that once posed a threat on mankind, can now be contained and destroyed before any other life threating symptoms arise.

Although modern medicine and creative medical practices have made tremendous advances in our nation, there is still one virus that has yet to been contained. It has been spreading across this country for generations, bringing about destruction and chaos, killing our people in various ways, just as heart disease, cancer, accidents, and suicide tend to do. This virus is identified as "Occulta Mortem" and is translated from Latin to mean "hidden death". The virus is responsible for a hereditary mutating disease referred to as "Financial Cancer" and 76% of adult Americans don't have a clue they are infected.

Irrational enough, it is possible to live in this plague-infested world and be safe from this cancer creating virus. Although it is deemed hereditary, and the majority of Americans are quietly suffering from this sickness, there is a prescription for this virus that can kill potent strands and suppress the mutation and growth of the virus. However, you must continue to use this prescription in full or the virus will flare up and could possibly lead to further complications, including death. This book was created to help save you from "Occulta Mortem"; it can save your life. Don't miss what may be your last lifeline.

I'M SORRY, YOU HAVE CANCER

"Breonna has cancer." I remember receiving a call from my mother, letting me know my sister was just diagnosed with Stage 3 Ovarian Cancer. Just a freshman in college, I can recall immediately dropping down to the floor, thinking I may lose my big sister. Although my sister was a former track athlete, ate fairly well, and had no real physical signs that would lead us to believe she was sick, the inside of her body was telling a completely different story.

That's the same story happening right now to you, your best friend, mother, father, teacher, coach, and even the one infamous rich guy or gal you know. Their exterior lifestyle is telling a different story than what is going on internally.

Again, the average American doesn't know they are financially sick and on their way to a financial death bed. Most will deal with this sickness for years until it finally consumes their thoughts, minds, and bodies and they completely shut down to die. The scariest thing is that this trait has been passed down from generation to generation but we have yet to acknowledge how serious this topic really is.

Imagine being diagnosed with cancer and telling the doctor you don't feel it's a big deal—informing him that you'll deal with it when you can, that you've been sick your whole life and your family is as well because those are the cards you were dealt. Sounds insane, right? Well, that's how crazy we sound when we look at our lifestyle and realize that we are in way over our head with bills and debt. We typically just shrug our shoulders and say, "this is the hand I was dealt. I have been poor my whole life, but at least I'm not as bad off as _____ (insert the friend's name you usually use)." The sad part is we judge our financial health and stability by comparing where we are in against people who are around us. Unfortunately, most of us have Financial Cancer and don't know its silently killing us.

FINANCIAL CANCER IS KILLING YOU

Whether you want to believe it or not I've been able to statistically and scientifically prove how financial cancer is the number one cause of death threatening illness in America. But let me stop you for a second because I know right now while you're reading this, you're going to probably say Jake has lost his mind there's no way that is possible that the lack of finances has any correlation to death in our communities. Listen, I get it I would think the same thing if I didn't know the facts. But I beg you to pay attention as you dive into the information that I have gathered for you, specifically in this chapter. I want you to open your mind to the statistical and scientific possibility that there is a chance that my hypothesis is correct and just maybe we have found a cure that can heal a lot of families, starting with yours in our communities.

Before we get started, I must Define to you what Financial cancer is. Financial cancer is my discovery therefore you will not find any other research or literary work on this specific concept. I developed the concept Financial cancer after I realized that there were four stages to financial cancer just like there are four stages to physical cancer you will find out more about that later in the book. However, what I did began to realize was Financial cancer does grow and interrupt or cause infection in other parts of our lives in ways that cancer grows and metastasizes in other organs inside of our body. Financial cancer is a compound effect of financial inefficiencies **(Debt)** that grow at unregulated and abnormal rates, thus causing chronic and acute stress that disrupts every aspect of your life.

Based on the statistics from the National Vital Statistics report volume 67, number 6 from the centers of

Disease Control and prevention (i.e. the CDC) I was able to uncover the top 5 causes of deaths amongst Americans.

Top 5 reasons of death amongst blacks:

Diseases of the heart 23.4%

Malignant neoplasms cancer 21.3%

Cerebral vascular diseases stroke 5.6%

Accidents unintentional injuries 5.5%

Diabetes 4.3%

Heart disease transpires when plaque buildup thickens and stiffens the artery walls. This buildup can inhibit blood flow through your arteries to your organs and tissues. Atherosclerosis is also most common cause of cardiovascular disease typically caused by correctable problems like high blood pressure or high cholesterol.

If you anything like my mom, she's always like hurry up and get to the point lol. I'm getting you there, I just need you to follow me briefly down this scientific journey, I promise it won't take long. I am trying to save your life here.

So, Jake, what does all of this have to do with financial cancer or money? That my friend is a great question and it will get answered right now. There is no secret that stress is one of the top complaints of adults old and young and the United States. The physical effects of prolonged stress are numerous, including a greater susceptibility to illness, a lack of energy, problems with sleep, headache, poor judgment, weight gain, depression, anxiety, and a host of other ills. Many people blame their inability to maintain healthy relationships on stress.

According to the American Psychological Association's last survey the number one cause of stress is money.

There's no guess that are several ways that chronic stress can kill you. When you stress it increases your levels of cortisol often referred to as stress hormone. Elevated cortisol levels interfere with learning and memory, lower immune function and bone density, increases blood pressure, cholesterol and leads to sure fight with heart disease.

So, the question is what is stress?

Stress is a measure of your mental and physical resistance to circumstances beyond your control. Stressors are threats, demands, or changes to which you attach special, significant importance, and with which you may struggle or feel uncertainty

Acute stress and chronic stress affect you in more ways than you think! When you encounter a stressful situation, stress hormones flood your bloodstream so that you can respond quickly and with strength. Watching your child nearly drown in water, for an example, might induce a hormonal response that enables you to catch your youngster before any harm is done. Specifically, your pituitary gland discharges ACTH (Adrenocorticotropic hormone) into the bloodstream, ACTH in turn, catalyzes the release of two Catecholamine Hormones, Epinephrine (Adrenaline) and none epinephrine or (non-adrenaline) from your sympathetic nerves into the bloodstream. Catecholamines, produced by the adrenal glands, serve as a neurotransmitter that signal the body to prepare for emergency action.

These psychological changes produce increased heart rate, breathing, blood pressure, and muscle tension that serves to supply adequate blood to your brain and musculoskeletal system. Higher levels of free fatty acids and blood sugars are released to provide immediate energy to survive the perceived emergency. This is what we call the well-known "fight or flight response".

It is the general absence of an emergency or threat taken in response to some stressor that may wreak havoc with your health. And most emotionally stressful social situations for example for those that result from financial worry you don't flee or fight instead you may "suck it up" and end up storing the stress internally. Additionally, your reaction to the stressor may include feelings of helplessness or fertility, which might cause stress hormones to continue to surge.

Long-term chronic stress can wreck your nervous system through cyclic adrenaline rush. It can cause oxidative damage to tissues in the body that leads to inflammation. It can stoke symptoms such as headache, achy neck, ulcer, allergies and diminished sexual desire. Eventually your body will adapt to a continued state of vigilance by producing an excessive amount of stress hormone cortisol. Too much stress, over time, can exhaust you (you burn out), your adrenal glands were cortisol is produced, and accelerate the aging process, harm your immune system and even shrink vital brain tissue resulting in memory loss and problems with concentration.

Dangerous cortisol levels is the leading but over often overlooked cause of insomnia and a major contributor to mental ills (depression, obsessive-compulsive and anxiety disorders), as well as physical disease is ranging from the common cold, recurrent herpes, obesity, and cancer. It is hard to think of any disease in which stress cannot play a precipitating or aggravating roll.

So, Jake, you are telling me that stressing over money over a long period of time can kill me?

Absolutely. acute stress is the leading cause of sudden death, especially in young healthy people with no evidence of coronary disease. But it can fail people at any age. Chronic stress causes heart disease. It is the secret cause of heart attacks and arterial disease -not fat or cholesterol. It contributes to high blood pressure or hypertension, a risk factor for cardiovascular problems such as heart failure and sudden cardiac death in a heart enlargement.

Feelings of helplessness when it comes to money leads to long-term depression and this significantly increases the risk of heart disease. Among other effects it triples the disease producing effects of smoking. Stress is the grim reaper that abruptly ends life by rupturing unstable plaque in a vital vessel or by triggering a little disturbance in heart rhythm.

Unfortunately based on the American Heart Association 2018, approximately 75% of black men and women develop high blood pressure by age 55 compared to 55% of white men and 40% of white women at the same age.

So because money is the number one cause for chronic and acute stress, and there are apparent links that connect people who are under severe psychological stress with picking up certain cancer creating behaviors, such as smoking, overeating, or drinking alcohol, it is safe for me to consider, conclude and hypothesize that in America Financial Cancer is the root cause for more Americans dying than any other cause combined.

Whew... Now I am out of breath, I said all of that to say, Financial Cancer has been killing our families for generations. Now that we know, we should start beginning to understand the importance of financial literacy in the African American community.

WHAT THE HECK IS STAGING?

Before I can give you the four stages of financial cancer, I must first breakdown and explain what "staging" is so you can get a better understanding of the parallelism between the two concepts.

Staging is a way of describing the nature of a cancer and how large it has grown. When doctors first diagnose a cancer, they carry out a multitude of tests to determine the size of the cancer as well as the location, and whether it has spread to surrounding tissues. They also check to see whether it has spread to another part of the body.

Before proceeding, let's first diagnose how bad your cancer may be. There are four key areas you must review before determining how bad your cancer is. The characteristics are as follows:

1. <u>STANDARDS OF LIVING</u>: What is your income in regards to your standard of living percentage? Here's an example of how to calculate your SOL:

a. *Total Home Gross Income (Married):*

$92,000 before taxes

$ 85,995.12 after taxes/12 months = MI

Monthly Income (MI): $6,454.78

    i. Cars: $958 (2 cars)

       Rent/Mortgage: $1200

       Home Owners Ins.: $135.45

       HOA Dues: $300

       Car Insurance: $216

       Utilities: $200

       Daycare: $1250

       Food: $275-$350

Total (SOL): $4609.45

Now we must figure out how much of your income is going toward you SOL. So, take your monthly income and divide it into your SOL (standard of living) and that should give you the percentage of income going toward your SOL. Look at the example below:

$$\frac{\text{Total SOL } \$4609.45}{\text{Monthly Income } \$6454.78} = .714 = 71.4\%$$

An example such as this is obviously not good; it is saying that 71.4% of your income is going to standards of living before any other debt, bills, or gas is paid. The scary thing is that for most Americans, this is a reality.

2. **SAVING FOR FUTURE: What percentage of your income are you giving to your future self? Take your monthly income and divide into the amount of money you invest or put aside for your future:**

Monthly Savings for Future: $250.00

Monthly Income   : $6454.78

$$= .0387 = 3.87\%$$

    a.   Retirement, investments, emergency funds, family trips

3. **FLEX MONEY: What percentage of your income are you spending on "flex money"?** *(Use the same formula that we used for SOL and future Savings):*   Flex Money: $$

                Monthly: $$

a. Entertainment, dining out, leisure activities, organizations, clubs, gym fees, side business costs.

4. **<u>SEED SOWING</u>: What percentage of your income are you spending on charitable donations?** *(Use the same formula that we used for SOL and future Savings):* Giving: $$

Monthly: $$

a. Church, Boys and Girls Club etc.

Please put your percentages in the blank table below you will need theses percentage to help you determine what stage you are in:

	STANDARD OF LIVING	FUTURE SELF	FLEX INCOME	GIVING
EXAMPLE	71.4%	3.87%	10%	13%
YOUR #S				

Using these tests for staging is very important because it helps your treatment team know which treatments you need. If a cancer is only in one location, a local treatment such as surgery or radiotherapy could be enough to get rid of it completely; a local treatment treats only one area of the body.

If a cancer has spread, local treatment alone will not be enough. You will need treatment that circulates throughout the whole body; these are called systemic treatments. Chemotherapy, hormone therapy and biological therapies are deemed systemic, as they circulate in the bloodstream.

The same way a doctor tries to locate the cancer and snip it out, you too must locate your cancer and do the same. However, because cancer can spread to the body and require systemic treatments, you may need to rid yourself of the all little cancers that may be eating up your income: eating out, excessive leisure time, large entertainment budget, high car payments. Drastic times call for drastic measures if you really want to beat this beast.

Staging Systems

Staging systems use the TNM system to divide cancer into stages. Most types of cancer have four stages, numbered from 1 through 4. Below is a brief summary of what each stage means for most cancers:

Stage 1

In stage one, the cancer is relatively small and contained within the organ it started.

Stage 2

In stage two, the cancer has not started to spread into surrounding tissue, but the tumor is larger than it began in stage one 1.

Stage 3

By stage three, the cancer is larger and may have started to spread into surrounding tissues.

Stage 4

Once the cancer has reached stage four, it has typically spread from where it started to another bodily organ. This is also called secondary or metastatic cancer. Here in this stage most patients only have 5 years to live after being diagnosed with stage IV cancer; 80% will probably live for at least another five years, and the other 20% would probably not survive this period of time.

Just as physical cancer has four stages, so does "Financial Cancer". The stages of financial cancer are based off a percentage system. Compare your income percentage in each of the given areas to know where you fall.

	STANDARD OF LIVING	FUTURE SELF	FLEX INCOME	GIVING
STAGE I	45% - 50%	5%	33%- 35%	10%
STAGE 2	53% - 57.5%	2%	33%- 35%	5.5%
STAGE 3	58%- 60%	0%	34%- 40%	1%
STAGE 4	62%- 66%	0%	34%- 40%	0%

On page 13, I gave a brief description of the stages of physical cancer. Now, in accordance with the chart above, here is the explanation of each stage of financial cancer.

Stage 1

In stage one, the financial cancer is relatively small, making the extraction of this malignancy moderately easy to fix if you can refocus and pay close attention to your spending habits.

Stage 2

In stage two, stress levels are rising and sleepiness nights are occurring increasingly. The financial cancer has not started to affect the flow of bills and activities being paid; however, the problem is larger than it was in stage one and you are probably looking at your budget knowing you are extremely close to having full blown cancer. The longer you wait to get ahead of this cancer, the worse it will become.

Stage 3

By stage three, you are living paycheck to paycheck. You are most likely experiencing high stress levels in your home, you and your significant other are arguing increasingly. Sleepless nights, are hardly the problem, it seems that rest is nowhere in your near future. You may be experiencing yourself getting more sick than usual and your mood is never constant. This is a red flag; your financial cancer is now larger and has started to spread. This is usually the tipping point, of alcoholism, drug addiction, botched marriages, and feelings of entrapment or worse thoughts of ending it all.

Stage 4

Once the cancer has reached stage four, this is what I call "the financial death bed." In this stage, most people only have 5 years to drastically change their habits or Occulta Mortem is sure to come. Marriages end, physical health takes a big dive, faith in God begins to come in question, and everything in your life seems out of order. The truth is only about 20% of the people diagnosed with stage IV financial cancer make it out unscathed.

What stage are you in? Did you know you were in that stage?

Acknowledging what stage, you are in will determine how hard you must fight to become financially healthy. I'm here to tell you, it's a hard road, but riding yourself of the cancer is possible.

Now that we've reviewed the stages of cancer, let's take a look at what financial health looks like:

	STANDARD OF LIVING	FUTURE SELF	FLEX INCOME	GIVING
OPTIMAL HEALTH	30%	30%	30%	10%
AVERAGE	37%- 40%	15%	33%- 35%	5.5%

Determining how far away you are from these standards will let you know how hard you must work to become financially healthy.

THE LONE RANGER

If you want to be strong, learn to fight alone.

-unknown

In recollection, my sister had to deal with a lot of emotions while going through chemotherapy; she felt alone, depressed, and, suicidal just to name a few. She knew we, as family, couldn't relate, and we knew we couldn't either. No matter who was there cheering her on, she knew this was a battle only she could face, and although it hurt, she ultimately had to go into the ring alone to face cancer. She had to deal with the harsh chemo treatments and its terrible side-effects like: weak stomach, shelled mind, and frail body just to name a few. Although we tried to empathize with her, we'll never truly understand the severity of the treatment and the toll it took on her body and psyche.

To some degree, these are similar emotions you will feel when you are going through Financial Chemo Therapy (FCT). No one will understand the sacrifices you must make to become financially healthy. You will have suicidal thoughts, want to quit, and often feel as though you have done enough. Your friends and family will be going out, but you must stay disciplined to your therapy so you don't lapse. You will be cash-strapped and without extra income to participate in leisure activities. You may also experience an array of emotions that you must learn to control; you can't let them get the best of you.

Luckily, there is a successful conclusion to this tale. Although my sister thought about quitting and giving up, she kept going and beat the evil cancer. You too will do the same if only you can see through to the finish line. Part II of this book is all about the two phases of the FCT. Getting through this tough therapy will not only suppress the virus and kill all financial cancer cells, but help you develop

wealthy habits, ultimately giving you the exact prescription

needed to achieve wealth. Nonetheless, before you

continue, finish giving yourself a true diagnosis, define

your stage, and determine your starting point.

What stage of Financial Cancer do I have?

_____

_____

_____

What is the first step I should take in riding my life of

Financial Cancer?

_____

_____

_____

_____

Part II
FCT

WE ARE AT WAR!

The two most powerful warriors are patience and time.

Leo Tolstoy

In the Luke 14:28-31, Yeshua was teaching his disciples about the importance of planning before acting.

> **28** "For which of you, wanting to build a tower, doesn't first sit down and figure out the cost, to see if he has enough to finish it?
> **29** Otherwise, when he has laid a foundation and isn't able to finish everything, all who see it begin to mock him,
> **30** saying, 'This man began to build and wasn't able to finish!'
> **31** "Or what king, going to make war against another king, won't first sit down to consider whether he is able with ten thousand to confront the one coming against him with twenty thousand?
> **32** If not, while the other is still far away, he sends an ambassador and asks for peace."

Just as Christ says in the scripture, a man who acts without a plan is foolish, will look foolish, and will be mocked for not being able to effectively complete the mission or task because he is not well planned. Christ then goes on to explain planning by using another example of a king going to war. He says, a king sits down and plans for a war against his enemy, but if he cannot win, he attempts to ask for peace.

The same goes for you in your war against financial health and wealth. If you are not well planned, you will be sure to fail. What separates an army from winning or losing is not necessarily based on how big ones' army is, but how planned ones' army is and how well the soldiers execute the plan. Execution is the number one reason a war is won or lost. So, planning to win is the first thing we must help you do. So in this phase of the book I will give you strategies and techniques that will give you the edge in killing off these financial cancer for good. However, learning about strategies and techniques alone are not enough to beat financial cancer indefinitely, applying the new information you gather is the only way that you can

beat this generation beast for good. Good luck on your

recovery, I hope to see you on the other side.

THE GAMEPLAN

Plans fail for lack of counsel,

but with many advisers they succeed.

Proverbs 15:22

On the road to financial health, you must next create a foundation on which your new economic principles will stand. Economic principles are simply your family's financial values or pillars. I like to call these the *non-negotiables*.

Most people unconsciously establish these rules in life, except when it comes to finances. Examples are as follows:

a. Bro Code

b. Girl Code

c. Family Behavior Code

d. Religious Preferences

We were born into most of these values, codes and or principles—our great grandmother passed down this hidden decree that included rules on how to act, how to speak, what to believe in, what school to attend, what sport to play; so on and so forth. Although these qualities may shape us in more good ways than bad, we must set some rules and boundaries that your family lives by no matter what!

All of this starts with one thing: a BUDGET! You must manage your finances like a bank and run your home like a business. Ask yourself, "if I oversaw a Fortune 500 company's financial budget, would I squander it all away on the things I currently waste money on?" The answer is probably NO WAY.

Again, use the table we discussed in Part I as a guide to better assist you and your family:

	STANDARD OF LIVING	FUTURE SELF	FLEX INCOME	GIVING
OPTIMAL HEALTH	30%	30%	30%	10%
AVERAGE	37%- 40%	15%	33%- 35%	5.5%

The income you make isn't just there for cars, shoes, and purses. You must also ask yourself, "if I were in charge of a business, would I spend 50 to 60 percent of my income on a building (office space), company cars, etc., or would I rather keep profit margins high." I think you would much rather choose the latter.

In developing your family's financial pillars, I would encourage you to reassess your spending habits. Remember: the whole goal is to run your finances like a bank and your home like a business. Be stingy; give your money away like a bank, rarely and with stipulations, but also be savvy; savvy enough to find ways to grow your home profits like a business.

Recommendations:

a. Hold Weekly Family Business Meetings (to go over weekly budget)

b. Find ways for everyone to bring in a stream of income ($1 -$100,000; everything counts)

c. Keep everyone goal driven; include your children in your financial goals because finances effect everyone.

d. Determine who your board members will be (this is typically a spouse and/or sibling). Also, decide what amount of money will be considered a big purchase. Before making any large purchases, take it to the board and get it approved.

CREATE A BUDGET

Understand your monthly budget should be assessed and may possibly change each month, so there should be a monthly, family, budget meeting held to ensure everyone is involved and aware of the month's budget. These are basic financial principles I help my clients create for their household and needless to say, it works wonders.

A common symptom that is found in all stages of financial cancer is the "out-of-sight, out-of-mind" symptom. The problem with this symptom is that it is so common for families to have this mindset that most don't see it as a root cause to developing initial stages of financial cancer. Lack of management when it comes to money, family, resources, relationships, marriages, talents, skills, as you know this list can go on and on; all end up down the same path, DESTRUCTION. So, managing and paying attention to the smaller details should not be an option but a must if you want to see yourself out of your current stage of financial cancer, and if you want to keep this disease away from your family for good. I'm a firm believer in whatever you don't pay attention to you lose. Whatever you don't value will soon depart from you and go to someone who does. Christ, in Luke 16:10 NLT, says "If you are faithful in the little things, you will be faithful in the large ones", so stop crying to God asking for increase when you don't know how to stretch and increase what you currently have.

Go back through your budget. Every dollar needs to be accounted for. If you don't want to do this by hand and keep up with everything on an excel sheet we have a budgeting tool that can help you with this process. You should keep your books for your personal finances like you a fortune 500 company and investors that you have to report to every quarter.

RUN YOUR HOUSEHOLD LIKE A BUSINESS

I see too many families that don't think of their job income as business revenue. The difference between successful business owners and the ones that fail, is a very thin line. On one side of the line is simply understanding the difference between revenue and profit. When a husband and a wife both bring into the household a yearly salary and don't equally think of their salaries like business revenue, they are sure to fail.

Revenue, by definition, means the total amount of money received from the sales of your products and services. Now, I know you're thinking, "Jake you are an idiot; I don't have a business that sells products or offers services". I would beg to differ, what do you think your job pays you for? They pay you for the services you offer. Which means, if they value the service you offer a lot, you get paid a lot. If they don't value your service as much, you don't get paid as much. When you begin to think that way your mind should begin to understand that all this time coworkers have been selling either their service or their product and you haven't realized. Ta-dah! You have been in business the whole time. Only stipulation is that the government doesn't fully see it that way, which is why you don't get the tax breaks that a business owner would; however, that's another discussion for another day. I just want you to think about the concept of running your home like a business.

So, example: Bob brings home $60,000 a year before taxes, and Sally brings home $60,000 a year before taxes. My question to you is: what is their household revenue? If you guessed $120,000 a year you are right, they own a 6 figure "revenuing" business (theoretically speaking). However, is that their profit for the year? If you answered "no" you are also correct. After taxes, household living, cars, cable, internet, electricity, insurance, activities, food, etc., most families are left with nothing, all because they don't budget, and they have no plan for future profits. If this were a real business, how serious would this family be in growing this income and creating more profit for the business? Exactly! They would be doing all they could to grow the business and cut cost in areas they don't need to be spending excess money. However, when it comes your household income, you don't hold yourself to the same standard you would if you ran a business. That's why most families fail at this simple strategy. All that to say: create a budget for your family and stick to it because your income and life depends on it.

GET A BOARD OF DIRECTORS

This part of your FCT is critical because of all the bad habits you've developed over time. Most people are ashamed to look at their financials themselves, let alone others. However, this is one elephant in the room you must address; if not, you will NEVER have a chance of getting better. Making more money is not the solution; setting financial non-negotiables is the initial key to purging the cancer.

When someone wants a successful business, they typically surround themselves with successful business owners, or people of influence that have succeeded in some degree to the level you want to achieve. A smart business owner would surround themselves with a board of directors or board of counsel. When it comes to succeeding and/or failing in life, most have no idea how important it is to surround yourself with people who are in the situations you want to be in. **Proverbs 28:26** says, "those who trust in their own insight are foolish, but anyone who walks in wisdom is safe." **Proverbs 24:6** says, "don't go to war without wise guidance; victory depends on having many advisors."

When it comes to your financial success you have to create a board of counsel or directors that you are accountable to. You need people that will give you wise counsel on the decisions you are making financially to help keep you grounded when emotions want to take you over. I know what you are thinking: Jake this is my money that I work hard for; I don't need someone to hold me accountable to my money! My question to you is: how far has that gotten you? I'm not encouraging you just to choose anyone, but I am encouraging you to chose someone that is right for you, someone you value, someone who is currently excelling and has your best interest at heart. Even if you have to pay someone for financial coaching, at least they have a financial tie to your success because it means they make more money when you do.

CHOOSE ROLES

Everyone in your family needs to have roles, especially the husband and the wife. Both of you can't be the CEO, CFO and the COO of the home. You have to decide who will be the CEO, the COO and the CFO. When everyone has a specific role in the home business, everything runs more smoothly. In my home, I am the CEO. I am the visionary for our family, I make the last decision after consulting our COO for her WISE counsel; however, it is still my job to lead the family in the right direction. My wife is the COO. She runs operations for our corporation and ensures the efficiency of our business. As for the CFO, my wife also has that title in our home, but it is shared with our tax, business advisor and myself being that I am in the financial industry. Every home is different. In one home, the wife may be the CEO and in other homes the roles may be flipped. That is something you have to work out to ensure the growth in your bottom line—profit.

KEEP EVERYONE GOAL FOCUSED

What are you guys working toward? Why do you exist as a family? What are you trying to accomplish together other than making a family and raising kids? You must dig deeper. All of this plays a role in how you budget and save. Typically, a family that does not save, budget or plan has no end goal. I can pretty much guarantee that if you knew what you were getting up for and going to work for, and what your family was fighting for, you would have a different approach to money, budgeting and finances. All of this is a part of game planning; figure out what you all are working toward. The union of two people is like the union of two business partners—there has to be more to the relationship than just I love you and you love me. What are you trying to accomplish? When you figure that out, budgeting and planning becomes so much easier whether you are single or in a relationship. Create little milestones that you want to hit, then celebrate only when you hit those milestones, to keep you focused on whatever you end goal is.

When will we, as a family, hold budget meetings?

_____

_____

_____

How will everyone contribute to the income?

_____

_____

_____

Who are our family's board members and what is each person's role?

_____

_____

_____

_____

_____

THE BIG PURGE

This phase of therapy is the biggest step and most crucial when moving toward financial health. Purging all the things that can be a negative influence to your therapy is similar to chemo; it's the worst part of therapy. Many people would prefer radiation; however, chemo must typically occur to get the result wanted.

For example, a recovering drug addict cannot be around drugs until he/she is fully free from the addiction, and even then, it is not recommended. I'm not telling you to go to the utmost extreme and completely rid yourself of everyone and everything in your life; however, you do have to eliminate all distractions for an allotted period of time. I would suggest you give both family and friends a heads-up and let them know that you will be in financial rehab for the next 3, 6, or 12 months and you won't be in contact as much.

You must purge yourself of anything that is taking away from your business (home) profits (home-business profits will be discussed in the next phase). Yes, sometimes this includes putting your ego aside and getting a cheaper car, removing fast food or restaurant visits from your routine, and doing your best to deter from getting all the name-brand clothes off the hottest rack; learn how to bargain shop. Remember, this isn't meant to last forever, but this does need to be for a significant period.

The biggest reason for the purge is to free up money that you are burning away so that you can do two things with it: save and buy down your debt. The first 6 months of the purge will be your hardest because you have to develop new habits and spending behaviors. However, your focus should be strong as long as you are focusing on your end goal and not paying attention to what's going on around you.

In the purge your first goal should be to save $1,000 in an emergency account. The reason why so many Americans pick up credit card debt is simply because they have no emergency account. If it makes sense to have a credit card in case of emergencies, wouldn't it make sense to have an emergency account in case of emergencies? Having an emergency is as important as having an IV during chemotherapy; it keeps your cashflow hydrated and nourished in case of any emergency or breakdowns that are out of your control. Seeing your emergency account build up will not only give you confidence but it will also give you a sense of comfort knowing that you are covered in case of an emergency. Play a game with your self: for every $500 you save in your account, you can take yourself out to you favorite restaurant within reason to celebrate. Once you began to do that on a consistent basis, you will want to raise the threshold to every $1000 saved. This strategy will keep you in high hopes as you are saving and buying down debt.

Make sure your immediate family understands the importance of compliance, and don't forget this one key concept: if you run your finances like a bank and your home like a business, financial health, security, and wealth will be a sure thing.

What will you purge first?

_____

_____

_____

_____

What will you purge second?

_____

_____

_____

_____

What will you purge third?

_____

_____

_____

_____

PROTECT YOUR #1 ASSET

Not every day is promised, and while you are on this journey to becoming free from financial cancer, none of us know what tomorrow may bring so protecting your number one asset is the definitely the most important step in this journey. What would happen if you started this journey to becoming free from financial cancer, and God forbid, you pass away or become sick and disabled? I can tell you, if you enter stage four of financial cancer, you won't come back from it.

What will happen to your family and all your hard work? In most cases, it would all be in vein, and the very thing you didn't want to happen, happens.

Now, the question you may be asking is, "Jake what is my number one asset"? Your number one asset is you and your ability to make money! There is no investment in the world that is more important than your ability to generate income for your family. If that income is not protected, then you really are playing Russian Roulette with your family's future. For a lot of people, when they think of life insurance, they think of it as being some type of burial expense; just meant to put you in the ground when its all said and done. Truth be told, that is one function for it, but that's not the only function and unfortunately, much of the country have a misconception about life insurance and how it works.

What if I told you car insurance only covered you if your car was totaled; how would you think about car insurance if you had to pay every month knowing that it only covered you if you totaled your car? You would probably think it was a waste, right? Because, there are so many other things that can happen to your car unexpectedly without it being totaled that you'd like to be covered for. Just like you get car insurance to cover you for the unexpected on all aspect of your car other than totaled, is the same reason you should get life insurance.

You can't control the unexpected heart attack, stroke, cancer, or organ transplant; all these things could send you to your financial death bed leaving your family financially devastated, even while you are still alive.

Well, the newest type of life insurance covers every aspect of your life, and with this type, you don't have to die to access it. If you become chronically or critically ill, you can be accelerated up to 80% of your death benefit while you are still living.

So, if you had a $1,000,000 policy, and you become critically ill, the insurance companies could send you up to $800,000 in a tax-free check while you are still living. In another instance, if you were to pass away, your family would receive the million-dollar death benefit to become fully free from financial cancer for several generations if planned properly. If you were to live and never get sick, you could access equity inside of your policy, tax free that you could use for anything like supplemental tax-free retirement, paying off the rest of your home, or paying the last of your consumer debt.

The #1 cause for bankruptcies in America is healthcare expenses for an unforeseen critical or chronic illness. But again, with the new type of life insurance, you are fully protected. Our company, Jake Tayler Financial, has partnered with billion-dollar, A+ rated insurance carriers that offer these new policies. Please contact us for a free consultation to see if you can be approved for this step.

FREEDOM ISN'T FREE. IT'S BOUGHT.

Now that you are protected. Let's get to the heart of the matter. 8 of 10 Americans are in debt. Debt is the new day slavery. Proverbs 22:7 say, "The rich rule over the poor, and the borrower is slave to the lender." I don't believe people realize that debt is the number one conversation in most marriages and households.

Debt is the cancer that most Americans openly allow to seep into their family's lives. More than 56% of all earned income goes to paying down some form of debt in more than 80% of American households. We are living in houses we really can't afford, buying cars that we really should not be driving, wearing clothes we really should not be wearing and taking trips that set our income back months and sometimes years. We are dedicating our lives to jobs and careers that do not serve us. 90% of Americans that work a job hate their current career or position. However, everyone that is in this 90% category not only have a fear of losing their job but are in fear of leaving because if they do and can't pay their debt and can potentially lose everything they have.

There are only 2 ways to get free in this world: either you die, or you buy your freedom. It's been the same way since actual slavery was created. You don't hope for freedom, you fight for freedom. Debt is the new age slavery and the sad part is that we all voluntarily put ourselves in bondage just because we don't want to be left out. We are so caught up in living in the now that we don't realize all of our bad habits are not only being passed down to our kids but eating our life away. We are serving the debt master 100% of our adult life working to pay both the debt master and the tax master, and not once do we ever say, "WAIT THIS DOESN'T MAKE SENSE; why am I borrowing money to live in a house and drive in a car I really can't afford"? Oh; and being able to make "payments" on these terrible debts does not constitute as being in your budget.

Paying you debt is more than just your way of building your credit. Paying your debt off is your true get out of slavery ticket. Think about it. You rather look nice, drive a nice car, and own a home you can't afford just to say you made it, then claim that you have all of these assets that don't make you money and technically you don't own—the bank does. At any time, the real owner of the property can come take it from you, especially the moment you are one payment late. You are not financially free, nor are you cancer free until you have control of your debts and you are debt free. PERIOD.

The strategy to becoming debt free is called "little target", also known as debt snowballing. Take all of your debt and you list them in order from smallest debt to biggest debt. After you list the debts from smallest to largest, the goal is to pay off your debt in order encompassing one small debt and then the next. After you pay off one debt, you take the full amount of the payment you were making and add it to the next debt on the list to pay the second debt off faster. You continue this until all debts are paid. Look at the picture diagram below to see how the debt game "little target" works.

All of this would be much easier if you had a debt elimination software you could plug your debt into, so it could track debt amounts, interest rates and keep record of you paying down your debts. If you need access to a debt elimination software, our company offers that solution for our clients. Please reach out to us to inquire

about solutions.

Solution: Little Target

AGE 35						
Retail Card 1	$220	+$220				
Credit Card 2	$353	$573	+$573			
Car Loan	$551	$551	$1,124	+$1,124		
Credit Card 1	$303	$303	$303	$1,427	+$1,427	
Mortgage	$1,293	$1,293	$1,293	$1,293	$2,720	$2,720
Total	$2,720	$2,720	$2,720	$2,720	$2,720	

23 years to pay off debt without this strategy and $214,442 in interest paid

Paid off in 9 years, Age 44 (14 years sooner) - Interest avoided $130,643

**(Age 44) Once debts are paid off, invest $2,720 each month at 9%
at Retirement... Age 67 = $2.4 million**

The fulfillment you will receive from paying off

your debt will be like no other. Paying off your debt, is

literally buying your freedom. Without this step you will

never become free from financial cancer. The only way

you can cure your family from the financial curse is to the

one that breaks it. Breaking the curse starts with you

becoming truly free from financial cancer. This may be the

one most important and hardest phase of your fight to

beating financial cancer.

INVEST IN YOU

A young boy aiming to become a painter will spend

countless hours studying, practicing and implementing

new techniques in order to one day produce a masterpiece.

Just as well, a young musician aiming to one day

perform on a grand stage will take the time to learn the

music theory, chord progressions, and many more

numerous musical techniques that will improve his/her

overall skills for them to release a piece of music that

many will sing and play along to.

Whether they know it or not, in both examples,

these individuals are doing one thing that will prove to be

the most valuable thing they may very well ever do in their careers.

They are investing in themselves.

Where you will stand and what new things you will be capable of doing tomorrow will largely depend on what you do to improve yourself today. Without working on ourselves and improving ourselves every day, it would be unrealistic for us to expect a much different future from the one we have right now. It would also be unrealistic for us to perform better in the future because we would be no different tomorrow from the person we are today.

That is why YOU are the most important thing you can place your time and money on.

An investment in yourself is a great example of self-love and may very well be the most profitable investment you will ever make. The worst thing you could do that would self-sabotage the 'future' you is continuing to do the same thing and assuming that you will automatically improve and advance to where you wish to be. That is definitely wishful thinking. No improvement in our lives will happen automatically without us working on them. If we want to get better, we must work on it.

No one is exempt from this fact.

Whether you are a powerful CEO wanting to expand your company and build your legacy, or an employee at the lowest point in the corporate ladder wishing to climb it faster, making yourself become more valuable to others around you will make you achieve those objectives.

When you are bold enough to take steps that will improve your performance and overall well-being, the universe will respond by granting you amazing results.

The effort you put into consistently investing in yourself will also play a large role in determining the quality of your life now and in the future.

What areas in your personal life can you do well to invest in? Consider the following.

Invest in your creativity

The highest form of Godliness is creativity; creativity is responsible for a lot of things in our lives. It allows us to have fun, it inspires us, and may very be what will change our life.

Do you remember when you were just a kid—how you were almost never bored when you were alone?

Do you know why? It's because your creative mind was at its highest peak and you had the power to bring anything to life to keep you company. Well that does not have to change. Our creativity doesn't have to diminish as we get older.

We can constantly set out time to deliberately work on creating something new. Spend an hour a day coming up with a business idea, improving an area in your work life, or improving your relationships; over time your creativity will be at its all-time peak.

Usually our best ideas don't form in crowded spaces, so take a walk or a hike and enjoy new sceneries; this will be a good investment in boosting your creative prowess.

Invest in your self-confidence

Confidence in yourself will take you places. Self-confidence will determine whether you stand up for yourself or not. It will determine whether you find the courage to leave all dysfunctional, cancerous, relationships or continue staying in one. It will make you act on your business plan or not. And it will mostly be the determining factor in whether you succeed or not.

So, find the time to invest in building your self-confidence. Learn to have the courage to speak your truth. The more you love yourself and own the value that you offer, the more confident you will become in sharing it with others.

Investing in your personal confidence is a great investment that will inspire others to do the same.

Invest in your knowledge

The more we learn, the more we realize that we have a lot more to learn. Educating yourself and gaining knowledge on a variety of things will empower you with tools that will make you and others become better. Author *Brandi L Bates*, feels this way about knowledge:

"Wrote my way out of the hood...thought my way out of poverty! Don't tell me that knowledge isn't power. Education changes everything."

Brandi L. Bates

Invest time in acquiring knowledge and then learning to apply that learned knowledge to help you stand apart from the crowd. Read books, listen to podcasts, and watch videos that add value to you as much as you can, for as long as you can. These are great resources that you can use to build your knowledge and expertise in any area.

Invest in your health

We can work for and get anything we want in life, but if we don't live long enough to see it and stay healthy enough to enjoy it, then it was of no use to us. Every day we grow older and with each passing day we have a chance to either build or break our health. Eat right each day, fueling your body with nutrients. When you focus on eating organic and healthier choices, you will feel better and have more energy.

Invest in personal exercise every day. This might not feel like it is that important when you're young and energetic, but your future body will thank you for the effort you put in now. Do something every day to get active and increase your heart rate, even if it's just walking the dog. Exercise will also give you the energy to take on the day with confidence because of how it makes you look and feel. Investing in your health will be an important investment for your personal gain.

Invest in your relationships

One thing we can't use an *'instant results'* business model on and expect it to flourish is our personal relationships. Relationships add more value to who we are and they take time to build. Your priceless, most valuable relationships won't take one day to build; they will take years, but they are also not built without putting in any effort.

We need to work on building them constantly, otherwise they will slowly fade and die off. This applies to business relationships as well. The benefits reaped from building our relationships can be measured and seen over their lifetime value. The more they grow, the more value they will have and the more valuable benefits you will see.

Invest in your finances

A lot of people say that money won't bring you any happiness, and that may very well be true, but you can't ignore the fact that being financially independent will give you the freedom to do the things you love a lot more. And those activities will bring a measure of fulfillment and happiness.

It does pay to be financially independent, that is why you must invest time in maintaining and managing your finances wisely.

As many financial planners will tell you, building wealth is a process made of many small actions that add up over time. So, if you want to see your bank account grow, getting healed from financial cancer is a must. Adopting new money and lifestyle habits now is a smart way to start.

Use this book as a jumpstart to snatching back control over your life. I don't expect you to read this book one time and be saved from all your bad habits and healed from your cancers. However, this book is a great way for you to start your journey to self-actualization.

Understanding the habits you've developed over the years that have gotten you to the current position you are in is the only way you will be able to truly start your journey to beating financial cancer once and for all.

I know you thought that I was going to talk about how to invest in stock, bonds, mutual funds and insurance vehicles in this section; but the truth is if your mind is not in the right place, if your relationships aren't in check, if you don't start to believe that you deserve to be financially independent and free from cancer, then no investing training in the world can help you become free. If your mind isn't in alignment with your heart, you won't have the discipline to overcome this disease and you too will be another person trapped and held captive to the ever so strong hold of financial cancer.

EPILOGUE

One divorce, an eviction, two brand new BMWs repossessed, a business that imploded right before my eyes and lost credibility amongst friends, family and clients, I've learned first hand about each of the stages of financial cancer. But I am here to tell you that I survived.

Teaching financial education for over 5 years, one would think I would have been able to see this cancer sneaking up on me but I didn't, much like you all. Like mentioned in part I, "The Plague", this cancer is like a plague; you don't realize you've fallen victim until it is too late. Trying to impress my friends and family and trying to keep up with "the Jones'" lead me down a dark road no one wanted to experience with me. God, blessed me in the midst of my mess; He helped me diagnose my sickness, and in the middle of my suffering, I found the cure. It cost me everything, but I found a cure.

This is a sickness most are unaware they are quietly suffering from. Even I, the "millennial financial specialist", fell sick to this deadly disease, because it doesn't happen all at once it sneaks up on you. But, I am here to tell you there is a bright light at the end of the tunnel, and I have the cure. Whether you are someone bringing in a six-figure income, an owner of a business, or struggling and feeling hopeless with no way out, I've been in every phase and can promise this first book of the wealth series, if used as a study manual, can break you free from cancer.

Final thoughts...

One of the most important phases in surviving financial cancer is for you to *"Invest in yourself"*. **If you don't, who else will?** You and only you must be proactive enough to take that responsibility.

Be yourself, and do what you can to make yourself the best you can be.

Investing in yourself emotionally, physically, spiritually and financially, will allow you to become the best version of yourself. The extent to which you invest in yourself, not only shapes the way you interact with the outside world, it often reflects the opinion you have of yourself and this will affect your chances of success in the future. Invest in yourself because your freedom depends on it.

"Your condition doesn't have to be your conclusion."

If you need help setting your **"HOUSEHOLD FINANCIAL PILLARS"** and putting a tailored **"PLAN IN PLACE"** to get you and your family out of financial cancer personally, visit **www.jaketaylerfinancial.com** and fill out the information under the tab **"Financial Cancer"** and I or one of my trained and licensed financial coaches will reach out to you for a consultation.

Made in the USA
Columbia, SC
10 June 2022